About the Author

Barton Cuong Williams was adopted from Vietnam Saigon in 1975 and raised in the eastern suburbs of Adelaide, South Australia. He has represented Australia in water sports, graduated as a school teacher and has written an award-winning international fitness programme for primary school children, as well as other children's picture books.

But What Are You?

Barton Williams

But What Are You?

Olympia Publishers
London

www.olympiapublishers.com
OLYMPIA PAPERBACK EDITION

A CIP catalogue record for this title is
available from the British Library.

ISBN: 978-1-78830-055-1

First Published in 2018

Olympia Publishers
60 Cannon Street
London
EC4N 6NP

Printed in Great Britain

Dedication

To all those children out there who have felt
left out or misunderstood.

Acknowledgments

Maria Fantis, Brian & Judy Williams,
Alex and Linda Fantis.

Hi, my name is Cuong.

I was born in Vietnam
during a war.

My mum and dad left me during the war so
I was sent to Australia as an orphan.

Soldiers put me in a
cardboard box so I could travel safely.

Hundreds of other babies were put into cardboard boxes and loaded onto planes.

When I arrived in Australia I met the Williams family. Maya Williams (Mum), Victor Williams (Dad) and Michael Williams (brother) all had light curly brown hair and blue eyes.
I have straight black hair and brown eyes.

"Your straight black hair is gorgeous," Mum would say every morning.
Mum would smile and give me hugs all the time.

I remember at kindergarten a boy snatched
a toy from me.
"Give it here, China-boy. What are you?"

I did not understand.

"Don't worry, Cuong, you're a good person and we love you!" Mum would say.

I joined the cricket team at primary school. "Hey, Cuong, what are you? Go play another sport. You don't fit in this team!" shouted a boy.

I did not understand.

"Don't worry, Cuong, you're a good person and we love you!" Dad would say.

One day I was at the shop with my brother Michael, when three boys stopped me.

"Hey, you, what are you? Go away!"
they shouted.
I did not understand.

"He's my brother! Now go away!"
replied Michael.

"He's your brother? He looks nothing like you!"
"Scram-jam before I get angry!"
shouted Michael.

The boys quickly left.
"Michael, what am I?"
"You're Cuong, you're a good person and we love you," Michael replied.

I have never forgotten that day at the shop. But what am I? I am Cuong, I am a good person and I have people who love me.